HILLARY RODHAM CLINTON

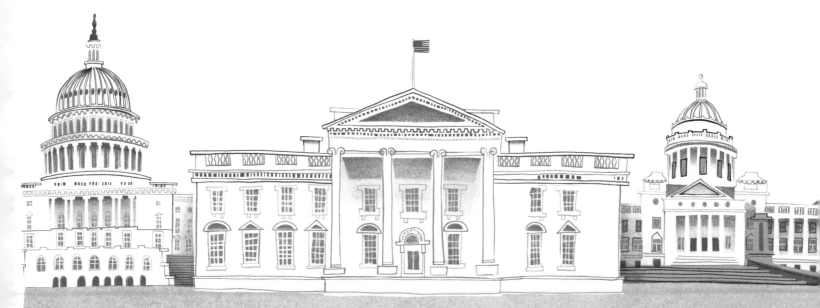

To the past and future leaders
of the fight for women's rights

—M.M.

To the women who work to change
the world a little every day,
To the girls who make the change worth it.

—L.P.

HILLARY
RODHAM CLINTON
Some Girls Are Born to Lead

By **Michelle Markel**   Illustrated by **LeUyen Pham**

BALZER + BRAY
An Imprint of HarperCollinsPublishers

In the 1950s, it was a man's world. Only boys could grow up to have powerful jobs. Only boys had no ceilings on their dreams.

Girls weren't supposed to act smart, tough, or ambitious. Even though, deep inside, they may have felt that way.

But in the town of
Park Ridge, Illinois,

along came
Hillary,

wearing thick glasses
and a sailor dress,
acing tests,

upstaging boys in class,

and lining up sports events
to raise money for the poor.

Take that, 1950s!
Some girls are born to lead,
and some love politics . . .

. . . and public service.

Through her church, Hillary learned about the troubled world beyond the green lawns and tree-lined streets of her town. Her youth group met with poor black and Latino teenagers in the inner city.

They went to hear a stirring speech by Dr. Martin Luther King, Jr. Do the most good you can, Hillary's youth minister taught. Be kind, work hard, aim high, her mother urged. They didn't tell her she could only go so far just because she was a girl.

There is nothing more tragic than to sleep through a revolution.

Hillary's hard work got her into a prestigious East Coast women's college.

Many of her classmates were brilliant prep school girls. But it was Hillary who got elected student body president and was chosen to give the first senior graduation speech the school ever had.

At the ceremony, a senator discouraged students from protesting about America's problems. Hillary was outraged.

When it was her turn, she approached the microphone and did a startling thing: she criticized him. Her classmates applauded for seven thunderous minutes.

After college, Hillary entered law school so she could work for justice. Most future lawyers were men, but that didn't scare her.

She trounced them in debates, attended rallies,

and helped start a newspaper about how laws could improve society.

That year the college was erupting
with violent demonstrations over civil
rights and a war in Vietnam.

When angry students and
professors met to discuss a strike,
who calmed everybody down?
Young Hillary, in her bell-bottoms,
sitting onstage, cool as can be.

On summer breaks, Hillary plunged into action. She investigated the filthy camps of migrant farm workers in Florida, where kids couldn't go to school or get medical care.

She walked up and down dangerous blocks in Texas, registering voters for the presidential election. One colleague called her "Fearless," and many friends thought so, too.

They thought Hillary would land a high-ranking job
in Washington, DC. But she didn't—

not yet.

Instead, she went to Arkansas to be with Bill, her law school sweetheart.

The two of them loved politics as much as they loved each other. They decided to spend their lives—and serve America—together.

When Bill ran and got elected to office,
Hillary did everything she could to help him.

She also became a mother,

worked at a top-notch law firm,

and advised groups dedicated
to children and the poor.

Hillary was a new breed,
a superwoman.

But sometimes it was hard, like when
she had to rush out of the courtroom to
call the babysitter about her sick child, or
when she heard the nasty things people said
about her looks, because she didn't take the
time to paint her toenails or style her hair.

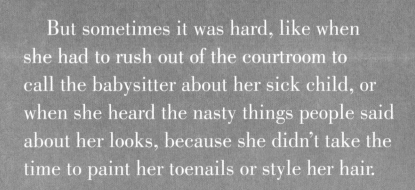

And it was hard for Hillary, a few years later, when she helped Bill campaign to become president of the United States.

She wasn't frightened of the crowds and cameras and reporters. But she couldn't believe how people criticized her—in ways they'd never criticize a man.

They said her headbands were too casual and her attitude was too feisty. An ex-president said a First Lady shouldn't be too strong or too smart. Others called her "the Hillary problem"—and a lot worse things than that.

It didn't matter what those people said—Hillary was determined to be an active First Lady.

"I love my husband and I love my country . . ." she stated. "I want to make a difference."

After Bill became president, Hillary led a task force on health care so all Americans could afford to see a doctor. Some people hated Hillary and her new ideas. When she went on tour to talk about her plan, she was met with mobs so threatening that she had to wear a bulletproof vest.

Hillary is tough as nails, news stories said. But after Congress turned down her health plan, she was crushed. She thought about Eleanor Roosevelt, another president's wife who tried to help the needy.

Go back to your knitting, I was told. Instead, I went back to work.

And so did Hillary.
She said her prayers, regained her strength—
and became a goodwill ambassador overseas.

In villages with dirt roads she heard heartbreaking stories of how baby girls were abandoned and young women were abused. She couldn't bear to be silent about such suffering.

At a United Nations conference in China, Hillary dared to say what no world leader was saying:

Her speech was blacked out by the Chinese government to try to stop her message from spreading. But the next day it made international front-page news.

At the end of Bill's term, Hillary finally got the chance to run for office herself, to become a US senator from New York.

She loved campaigning across the state, getting to know the people in its cities and small towns and farms. Though the odds were against her, she won the race. No First Lady had ever done such a thing.

After taking office, Hillary worked long, tiring days for all New Yorkers. She fought hard for funding to help the firefighters and first responders who got sick after the attack on September 11.

Hillary wanted to serve her country—every bit of it. America was hurting. Thousands of people were losing their jobs, homes, and medical care.

So in 2007, at age fifty-nine, Hillary joined the race to be a candidate for president. Reporters and opponents made fun of her age, her laugh, her legs, her ambition—she knew they would.

But she kept fighting—and though it was not enough to win, she earned a record-breaking 18 million votes.

During her concession speech, Hillary said those votes were 18 million cracks in the glass ceiling—the hard, invisible prejudice that prevents women from becoming powerful leaders. Standing proudly at the podium, she declared,

It's unremarkable to think that a woman can be the president of the United States, and that is remarkable!

Hillary returned to the Senate—
but not for long. President Obama,
her former rival, wanted her to be
his secretary of state.

The woman who was called too ambitious now met
with kings, sultans, and prime ministers—in a total of 112
countries. She visited activists to draw attention to their
causes. Wherever she went, her message was the same:

"The role and rights of women, their freedom and equality and dignity, is the unfinished business of the twenty-first century."

No one gets to stop a girl from being the greatest person she can be. Hillary thinks everyone deserves that chance. All her life she's fought for fairness and compassion. The cruelest words and wrongest barriers have not been strong enough to hold her back.

No matter what Hillary does next, if she wants
to change the world, she'll find a way.

TIMELINE

1947 Hillary Rodham is born in Chicago, Illinois.

1950 The Rodham family moves to Park Ridge, Illinois.

1955 In Alabama, Rosa Parks is arrested for refusing to give up her seat in the front of a bus. To protest segregation, the black community holds a yearlong bus boycott, led by Dr. Martin Luther King, Jr. The modern civil rights movement gains momentum.

1962 Minister Don Jones takes Hillary's church youth group to Chicago to hear a speech by Dr. Martin Luther King, Jr.

1965 Hillary graduates from Maine Township South High School, and in the fall she attends Wellesley College in Wellesley, Massachusetts.

Students for a Democratic Society (SDS) and the Student Nonviolent Coordinating Committee (SNCC) begin the first of several marches protesting the Vietnam War. In the coming years, the antiwar movement grows.

1966 Betty Friedan and other activists form the National Organization for Women (NOW) to promote full equality of the sexes.

1969 In the spring, Hillary graduates from Wellesley and becomes the first student to give a commencement address. *Life* magazine publishes her photo along with an excerpt of her speech, in which she criticizes Senator Edward W. Brooke.

In the fall, Hillary attends Yale Law School in New Haven, Connecticut. She is one of 27 women in a class of 235. During her time there, she serves on the editorial board of the *Yale Review of Law and Social Action* and works at the Child Study Center.

1970 Yale students protest the unfairness of a murder trial involving nine members of the Black Panther Party.

1971 Hillary goes to Washington, DC, to work on Senator Walter Mondale's subcommittee on the housing, education, sanitation, and health of migrant workers.

1972 Hillary works on Senator George McGovern's presidential campaign.

1973 Hillary receives her law degree from Yale and begins work as an attorney for the Children's Defense Fund.

1974 Hillary serves on the staff of the House Judiciary Committee investigating criminal charges against President Richard Nixon. She also teaches at the University of Arkansas School of Law.

1975 Hillary marries Bill Clinton.

1978 When Bill Clinton is elected governor of Arkansas, Hillary becomes the state's First Lady. She also works as the first female chair of the Legal Services Corporation.

1979 Hillary becomes the first female partner at Rose Law Firm.

1980 Hillary gives birth to daughter Chelsea Clinton.

1982 The Equal Rights Amendment, originally passed by Congress in 1972, fails to be ratified by the necessary number of states. The amendment would have guaranteed equal rights for women.

1983 Hillary chairs the Arkansas Educational Standards Committee.

1992 Bill Clinton is elected as the forty-second US president.

1993 When Bill Clinton is sworn in as president, Hillary becomes the First Lady. The president appoints her chair of the Task Force on National Health Reform.

1995 Hillary visits South Asia, where she promotes human rights. She speaks out for equal rights for women at the UN Fourth World Conference on Women in Beijing, China.

1996 Bill Clinton is elected to a second term as president.

2000 Hillary is elected to the US Senate from New York. She is the only First Lady to have run for public office.

2001 As part of a coordinated terrorist attack, two hijacked jetliners crash into and destroy the World Trade Center in New York City. Exposure to toxic debris causes illness to residents and workers in Lower Manhattan.

2006 Hillary is reelected to the US Senate from New York.

2007 A financial crisis begins, causing evictions, foreclosures, and unemployment.

2008 Hillary competes in the race to be the Democratic nominee for president. She wins more primaries and delegates than any other female candidate in history. Barack Obama is elected the forty-fourth US president.

2009–2013 Hillary serves as the sixty-seventh secretary of state.

2013 Through the Clinton Foundation, Hillary launches No Ceilings: The Full Participation Project. The initiative will evaluate the progress women and girls have made since the UN Fourth World Conference on Women in Beijing in 1995.

2015 Hillary announces her candidacy for president.

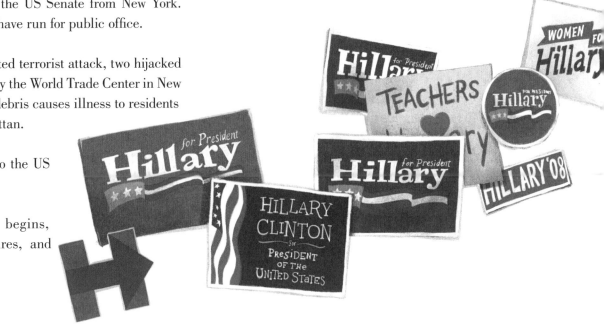

ARTIST'S NOTE

Illustrating a book on Hillary Rodham Clinton is no easy feat. The number of biographies I've read, articles I've gone over, people I've spoken to, and notes I've had to keep straight is staggering to say the least, and I've done my best to incorporate as much of all that as possible into each illustration. From conversations with the charming Clinton House Museum director, Kate Johnson, to Hillary's generous college classmate Laura Grosch, I found myself growing ever more admiring of Ms. Clinton and her many accomplishments. Charting the life of Hillary Clinton is like charting the growth of the role of women over the past fifty years. The truth is, this amazing woman has broken so many barriers in her lifetime that I know without her, my life and the lives of many professional women today would simply not be the same. And I, for one, will be eternally grateful.

—LeUyen Pham

Pages 4–5 — Well-known personalities of the 1950s: inventors of Bell Solar Battery, 1. Gerald Pearson, 2. Daryl Chapin, 3. Calvin Fuller; entertainers 4. Bing Crosby and 5. Bob Hope; 6. Vice President Richard Nixon; 7. General James Van Fleet; 8. singer Elvis Presley; 9. singer Buddy Holly; 10. pilot Neil Armstrong; "The Big Four," 11. British prime minister Anthony Eden, 12. French prime minister Edgar Faure, 13. US president Dwight Eisenhower, 14. Soviet minister of defense Nikolai Bulganin; 15. chef Fernand Point; 16. Chairman Mao Tse-tung of China; 17. violinist Ivry Gitlis; 18. explorer Jacques Cousteau; 19. playwright Samuel Beckett; 20. ballplayer Mickey Mantle; 21. Israeli prime minister David Ben-Gurion; 22. Soviet premier Nikita Khrushchev; 23. entertainer Nat King Cole; 24. journalist Edward R. Murrow; 25. playwright Tennessee Williams; 26. physicist Albert Einstein; 27. Nobel Laureate Albert Schweitzer; 28. ballplayer Jackie Robinson; 29. businessman Walt Disney; 30. inventor of the laser, Gordon Gould; 31. artist Jackson Pollock; 32. young Hillary Rodham, age eight.

Page 7 — Hillary's neighborhood friends ran mock Olympic games to raise money for the United Way (left to right): Rawls Williams, Hillary Rodham, Kris Dernehl, United Way representative, Gordon Williams, Suzy O'Callaghan Lorenz, Hugh Rodham, photographer, Hillary's pet cat Isis.

Pages 8–9 — Accompanied by her minister and lifelong confidante, Don Jones (pictured far right), Hillary and her youth group were in attendance when Martin Luther King, Jr., delivered his speech "Remaining Awake Through a Revolution" at Chicago's Orchestra Hall in 1962.

Page 10 — Hillary and her classmates leaving Tower Court at Wellesley College (left to right): Eleanor Acheson; Karen Williamson; dorm mate and artist Laura Grosch; Hillary's "Big Sister," Shelley Parry; *Ethos* founders Janet McDonald and Francille Wilson; Hillary Rodham.

Page 11 — Senator Edward W. Brooke is seated to the far right. Senator Brooke was the first African American to be popularly elected to the United States Senate, in 1966.

Page 12 — Top image: Hillary with her fellow Yale Law School Barristers Union classmates during a mock trial. Shown here are Rufus Cormier, Jeff Rogers, Bob Alsdorf, Hillary Rodham, Dan Johnson, Bill Clinton, D. Golub, and Tony Rood. Lower right image: Hillary on the editorial board of the *Yale Review of Law and Social Action*.

Page 13 — Yale May Day rallies. In the crowd at the bottom is Professor Charles Reich, author of *The Greening of America*.

Page 14 — Top image: Hillary was awarded a grant to work at Marian Wright Edelman's Washington Research Project. Ms. Edelman is also the founder of the Children's Defense Fund. Bottom image: Hillary with her fellow volunteers Betsey Wright and Sara Ehrman on the streets of San Antonio, Texas.

Page 15 — Top image: Hillary and her fellow impeachment inquiry staff (left to right): Bernard Nussbaum, Joe Woods, Representative Barbara Jordan, John Doar, Hillary. Bottom image: Hillary with Sara Ehrman in her VW Bug, driving down to Arkansas. Ms. Ehrman spent the entire drive trying to convince Hillary not to give up her career to be with Bill Clinton.

Page 16 — Bill and Hillary's wedding (clockwise from upper left): Hillary's parents, Hugh and Dorothy Rodham; Hillary and Bill; Bill's mother, Virginia Clinton Kelley, pastor Vic Nixon and his wife, Freddie; old classmate Johanna Branson and childhood friend Betsy Johnson Ebeling; Bill's brother, Roger Clinton; Richard B. Atkinson.

Page 17 — Top image: Bill and Hillary with gubernatorial campaign manager George Shelton, who passed away before Bill Clinton was president. Third image: Hillary with her good friends and coworkers at the Rose Law Firm, Vince Foster and Webb Hubbell. They later both held positions in the Clinton administration. Bottom image: Hillary cofounded the Arkansas Advocates for Children's Families.

Page 18 — Hillary is seen running from the Pulaski County courthouse in Arkansas.

Page 19 — In the audience are Daniel Wattenberg of the *American Spectator*, who labeled Hillary Rodham Clinton "Lady Macbeth," and David Brock, who wrote the story about Troopergate, a scandal that greatly affected the campaign.

Page 20 — Hillary is reading an article called "The Hillary Problem," a story by William Safire that originally appeared in the opinion pages of the *New York Times*. The man styling her hair is her hairdresser, Christophe Schatteman.

Page 22 — Hillary on tour with the Health Security Express, a nationwide bus tour on health reform.

Page 23 — In this fanciful imagining of her role model Eleanor Roosevelt, Hillary is pouring tea with a special pot given to her as a gift at the Lamp Lighter Café in Belfast by a group of Irish women leaders of the peace movement. The two are seated in the East Sitting Hall of the White House.

Page 24 — Bottom image: Hillary and Chelsea visiting a Pakistani village during their 1995 visit through South Asia. The trip was at the behest of the US State Department in an effort to improve relations with India and Pakistan.

Page 26 — Hillary's New York senate campaign strategy included a "listening tour," in which she visited nearly every county in the state of New York. The cities seen here are East Aurora, Ithaca, Oneonta, Granville, and Cooperstown.

Page 28 — Hillary, Bill, and Chelsea are seen here at the city hall in Manchester, New Hampshire, where Hillary won the Democratic primary over Barack Obama.

Page 30 — Bottom image: Hillary is depicted with several world leaders (left to right): Benjamin Netanyahu of Israel, Nicolas Sarkozy of France, Aung San Suu Kyi of Burma, David Cameron of England, Wen Jiabao of China, Nelson Mandela of South Africa, Hamid Karzai of Afghanistan, Hosni Mubarak of Egypt, Angela Merkel of Germany, Ellen Johnson Sirleaf of Liberia, Mahmoud Abbas of Palestine, Oscar Arias of Costa Rica.

Page 31 — The winners of the International Women of Courage Award granted during Hillary's tenure as secretary of state: (top row) Julieta Castellanos (Honduras), Nirbhaya "Fearless" (India), Maryam Durani (Afghanistan), Jestina Mukoko (Zimbabwe), Fatima Toure (Mali), Dr. Lee Ae-Ran (Republic of Korea), Agnes Osztolykán (Hungary); (second row) Jineth Bedoya Lima (Colombia), Samar Badawi (Saudi Arabia), Tsering Woeser (Tibet), Malalai Bahaduri (Afghanistan), Androula Henriques (Cyprus), Ann Njogu (Kenya); (third row) Sister Marie Claude Naddaf (Syria), Eva Abu Halaweh (Jordan), Zin Mar Aung (Burma), Yoani Sánchez (Cuba), Hawa Abdallah Mohammed Salih (Sudan), Roshika Deo (Fiji); (fourth row) Şafak Pavey (Turkey), Solange Pierre (Dominican Republic), Nasta Palazhanka (Belarus), Shadi Sadr (Iran), Aneesa Ahmed (Maldives); (fifth row) Officer Pricilla de Oliveira Azevedo (Brazil), Guo Jianmei (China), Shad Begum (Pakistan), Henriette Ekwe Ebongo (Cameroon); (sixth row) Fartuun Adan (Somalia), Jansila Majeed (Sri Lanka), Tạ Phong Tần (Vietnam), Razan Zaitouneh (Syria), Hana El Hebshi (Libya).

Pages 32–33 — Well-known personalities of today: 1. entertainer Barbra Streisand; 2. author J. K. Rowling; 3. chemist Ada Yonath; 4. anthropologist Jane Goodall; 5. entertainer Madonna; 6. singer Aretha Franklin; 7. writer Arundhati Roy; 8. poet Maya Angelou; 9. writer Alice Munro; Supreme Court justices 10. Sonia Sotomayor, 11. Ruth Bader Ginsburg, 12. Elena Kagan; 13. Burmese leader Aung San Suu Kyi; 14. Argentine president Cristina Fernández de Kirchner; 15. physicist Lisa Randall; 16. actor/humanitarian Angelina Jolie; 17. astronaut Kathryn D. Sullivan; 18. actor Meryl Streep; 19. journalist Christiane Amanpour; 20. activist Gloria Steinem; 21. chef Alice Waters; 22. activist Mother Teresa of Calcutta; 23. US secretary of state Condoleezza Rice; 24. Brazilian president Dilma Rousseff; 25. German chancellor Angela Merkel; 26. British prime minister Margaret Thatcher; 27. Pakistani prime minister Benazir Bhutto; 28. General Motors CEO Mary Barra; 29. PepsiCo CEO Indra Nooyi; 30. photographer Cindy Sherman; 31. Liberian president Ellen Johnson Sirleaf; 32. philanthropist and media mogul Oprah Winfrey; 33. artist Marina Abramović; 34. athlete Serena Williams; 35. Pakistani activist Malala Yousafzai; 36. Indian National Congress president Sonia Gandhi; 37. Hillary Rodham Clinton; 38. US secretary of state Madeleine Albright.

SELECTED BIBLIOGRAPHY

Bernstein, Carl. *A Woman in Charge: The Life of Hillary Rodham Clinton.* New York: Knopf, 2007.

Chafe, William H. *Bill and Hillary: The Politics of the Personal.* New York: Farrar, Straus and Giroux, 2012.

Clinton, Hillary Rodham. *Hard Choices.* New York: Simon & Schuster, 2014.

———. *Living History.* New York: Simon & Schuster, 2003.

———. *It Takes a Village: And Other Lessons Children Teach Us.* New York: Simon & Schuster, 1996.

Gerth, Jeff and Don Van Natta Jr. *Her Way: The Hopes and Ambitions of Hillary Rodham Clinton.* New York: Little, Brown, 2007.

Sheehy, Gail. *Hillary's Choice.* New York: Random House, 1999.

Hillary Rodham Clinton: Some Girls Are Born to Lead

Text copyright © 2016 by Michelle Markel

Illustrations copyright © 2016 by LeUyen Pham

All rights reserved. Printed in the United States of America.

No part of this book may be used or reproduced in any manner whatsoever without written permission except in the case of brief quotations embodied in critical articles and reviews. For information address HarperCollins Children's Books, a division of HarperCollins Publishers, 195 Broadway, New York, NY 10007.

www.harpercollinschildrens.com

Library of Congress Cataloging-in-Publication Data

Markel, Michelle.

  Hillary Rodham Clinton : some girls are born to lead / Michelle Markel ; illustrated by LeUyen Pham. — First edition.

        pages   cm

    Audience: K to grade 3.

    ISBN 978-0-06-238122-4 (hardcover : alk. paper)

    1. Clinton, Hillary Rodham—Juvenile literature.   2. Presidents' spouses—United States—Biography—Juvenile literature.   3. Women cabinet officers—United States—Biography—Juvenile literature.   4. Cabinet officers—United States—Biography—Juvenile literature.   5. United States. Department of State—Biography—Juvenile literature.   6. Women legislators—United States—Biography—Juvenile literature.   7. Legislators—United States—Biography—Juvenile literature.   8. United States. Congress. Senate—Biography—Juvenile literature.   9. Women presidential candidates—United States—Biography—Juvenile literature.   10. Presidential candidates—United States—Biography—Juvenile literature.   I. Pham, LeUyen, illustrator.   II. Title.

E887.C55M367   2016

352.2'93092—dc23

[B]

2015006604

CIP

AC

Typography by Dana Fritts

16 17 18 19   WOR   10 9 8 7 6 5 4 3 2

❖

First Edition